THIS
HIGH FIVE HANDBOOK
BELONGS TO:

_____

THE

HIGH FIVE

HANDBOOK

BY
THE HAND & KNUCKLE SOCIETY

KNOCK KNOCK
VENICE, CALIFORNIA

Published by Knock Knock
1635-B Electric Ave.
Venice, CA 90291
knockknockstuff.com
Knock Knock is a registered trademark of Knock Knock LLC

ISBN: 978-160106845-3
UPC: 825703-50225-1

TABLE OF CONTENTS

WELCOME

We are the Hand & Knuckle Society: a clandestine organization of individuals who believe in the power of the pound, the significance of the shake, and the supreme holiness of the high five.

You don't know our members, but you've met us before. Remember that time you connected on a perfectly timed double-handed high five with a fellow fan at the stadium? One of us. Recall that perfectly negotiated four-way traffic stop where a few simple waves made your day? That was us, too. Still haunted by that awkward moment when you weren't sure if you should hug or handshake? Not one of us—we'd never let that happen.

We have spent generations covertly ensuring good greetings happen daily. In other words, we are like Fight Club, but with more fist bumps than fisticuffs. And we wear shirts much more often.

But it is time we come out of the shadows. Today's culture has forced us to go public. The speed of change and dominance of technology have changed the way people communicate. This is a world with more social networks than

Ferientes manus loquimini veritatem

(Slapping hands speak the truth)

—The Hand & Knuckle Society Motto

---

socializing, where web chats replace actual chats, and emojis replace our true emotions. Our fast-paced life has resulted in fewer and fewer real-life human exchanges. And more and more loneliness.

What a sad, sad world it would be with no waves, no nods, and no hugs. No bumps. No daps. No up-highs. No down-lows. No, we can't stand by and leave society hanging.

So we cracked our fist-bumping knuckles and wrote this book.

We want everyone to reconnect with connecting. To say what's up to what's up. To high five the high five again.

This is our inspiration.

This is our cause.

And this is our book.

HIGH FIVE COMMANDMENT NO. 1
"THE HANDS SHALL SPEAK WHAT THE MIND THINKS."

CHAPTER 1

HANDS & SIGNS

"Talk to the hand." Despite the contemptuous connotation of this phrase, we make it our mantra. Because hands really can talk, whether the face is listening or not.

The human hand is one of the most complex, versatile, and beautiful pieces of engineering in all of nature. A multitude of bones, tendons, nerves, fingers, plus an opposable thumb work together to perform the most useful of tasks (like holding loved ones and writing sonnets) and the most useless of tasks (like thumb wrestling and jazz hands).

Our hands can say a lot (and we're not even talking about American Sign Language). We just need to know how to hear them with our eyes. While that sounds complicated, knowing how to communicate with your hands through signs and waves is actually quite simple.

WHAT IS THE HAND?

In literal terms, our hands are the prehensile extremities of the superior limb, or those funny looking multifingered things at the end of our arms.

In more metaphorical terms, hands are a portal to humanity, an amalgamation of senses, skills, emotions, and cultures. They hold the power to change the world. In other words, hands are pretty freakin' important.

The human hand is unique in the animal kingdom. Next time you shake hands with a Central African Chimpanzee, you'll notice that while similar, human hands have evolved in one key area. As the *Journal of Anatomy* not-very-simply puts it, "the thumb metacarpal articulates with the carpals in a saddle joint which in combination with remodelling in the metacarpal—phalangeal joint allows its distal pad to be placed against those of the other fingers, providing full opposability." In case you weren't an anatomy major, that means our thumbs move freely and work with our fingers to pick stuff up.

This freaky little finger trick allows us to manipulate tools, throw weapons, and do a variety of complicated and precise things most other animals can't. (Take that, bears!)

So get ready to throw your hands in the air, learn more about these amazing appendages, and become a true player.

WHAT'S THE HAND MADE OF?

The hand is a wonderful nexus of tissues arranged in three main areas:
1. the heel, 2. the palm (volar/opistenar), 3. the digits (fingers and thumb).

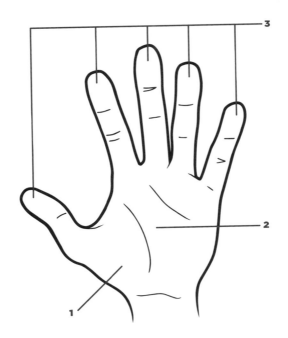

'SUP WITH FINE MOTOR SKILLS?

About a quarter of the motor cortex in our brain is dedicated entirely to the muscles used to work our hands. In case you weren't sure, that's the part of the brain that controls every single movement our body can make, except sneezing with our eyes open.

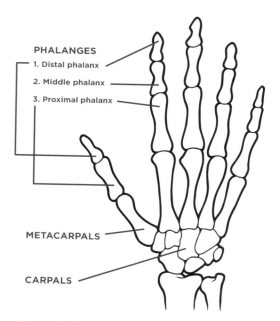

PHALANGES
- 1. Distal phalanx
- 2. Middle phalanx
- 3. Proximal phalanx

METACARPALS

CARPALS

The hand is attached to the arm by the wrist and comprised of:

- ☞ 27 bones: 8 in the wrist (aka carpals), 5 in the palm (aka metacarpals), 3 per finger and 2 per thumb (14 phalanges)
- ☞ 29 joints: including knuckles
- ☞ 35 muscles: 17 in the palm, 18 in the forearm
- ☞ a boatload of ligaments, nerves, and arteries

'SUP WITH CRACKING KNUCKLES?

Forget what your grandma said—you won't get arthritis from cracking your knuckles. The cracking sound actually comes when a bubble forms in the fluid between the bones of the knuckle joint. Recent studies suggest that cracking your knuckles might actually be good for the joints and cartilage—so crack away.

THE DIGITS

Now that you have a grasp of your hands, it's time to focus on your fingers in all their glory. Read on for a rundown of your digits and what message they might be sending.

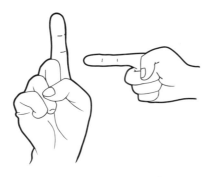

=== INDEX FINGER ===

aka: digitus secundus, *forefinger, pointer, trigger finger, lickpot*

The first and most prominent of the four fingers, our forefinger is typically both the most dexterous and celebrated of the bunch— like the star quarterback of the team. Although it competes with the ring finger in length, its pivotal role in mouse-clicking, attention-pointing, and all-around thing-poking is undeniable. As a communicator, it has a lot to say.

Things it could mean:

- ☞ Come here.
- ☞ Wait a second.
- ☞ We're number one!
- ☞ Taxi!

- ☞ Table for one.
- ☞ Look, over there!
- ☞ Oh, no you didn't! (when wagged)

MIDDLE FINGER

aka: digitus medius, *the third finger, the bird, the finger*

Typically the longest of all the fingers, our third finger is
the rock star of the bunch. It is perhaps the most famous
finger in the western world, and is a widely recognized form
of insult ubiquitously known as "giving the finger."

Things it could mean:

- [Vulgar insult]
- ... and the horse you road in on.
- Stop looking at me.
- Sit and spin.
- Hey, watch where you're driving!
- Up yours!

'SUP WITH FINGER MUSCLES?

Fingers don't have any muscles. The flexor muscles
(they bend the finger joints) and extensor muscles
(they straighten 'em back) are in our palms and forearms.
They're connected to the finger bones by tendons,
and move our fingers like meat marionettes.

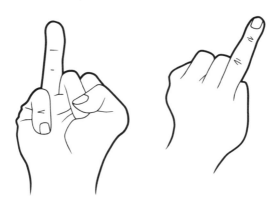

RING FINGER

aka: digitus medicinalis, *the fourth finger,*
the ringer, my precious

The ring finger is a reliable digit. Today, it spends much of its
time in the shadow of the middle one. But in ancient times, it
was believed that a magical vein ran straight from your heart
to the fourth finger on your left hand. That's why it became
tradition to wear the wedding ring on that finger.

Things it could mean:

☞ Put a ring on it!
☞ I want to flip you off but that's wrong, so here's the loophole.
☞ My index finger is currently busy but I still need to point.

'SUP WITH RING FINGERS IN JAPAN?

An oddly specific question, but the answer is your
sister. In Japanese Sign Language, the middle finger
means brother and the ring finger means sister.

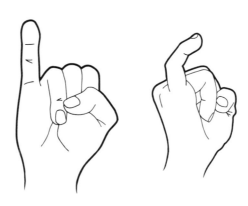

LITTLE FINGER

aka: digitus minimus manus, *the fifth finger, baby finger, pinky, lil' pink*

Our outermost finger is definitely the runt of the group. It has a limited range of motion and, aside from the occasional nose scratch, is seldom used on its own. Unnecessary as it may be, there is no denying the agreement it binds when locked with another (pinky swear!).

Things it could mean:

- 🤙 You, sir, are not well endowed.
- 🤙 I'm a fancy tea drinker.
- 🤙 One meeeeellion dollars! (when brought to mouth)
- 🤙 Promise!

'SUP WITH THE LITTLE ONES?

While the index and middle fingers are designed for detailed tasks, the pinky actually carries more weight when you grip something. Try doing a pull-up without using your pinky fingers versus without using your index fingers. Score one for the little guys.

THUMB

aka: digitus primus manus, *pollex, thumbkin, the other Mr. T*

Our first digit is also our most important. Its movements are so complex we can't even call it a finger. And just like abstract thought, neuroscience, and the hokey pokey, the fully opposable thumb is one of those things that separates us humans from other animals.

Things it could mean:

☞ Cool!
☞ I need a ride.
☞ Get outta here!
☞ Yes. (when up)

☞ No. (when down)
☞ This guy! (when pointed at self)
☞ Aaaay! (when Fonzie)

'SUP WITH CAESAR?

Back in the day, Roman Emperor Julius Caesar reportedly ordered the thumbs—or some say, the hands— of all his captured enemies be cut off so they would not be able to bear arms against him ever again.

THE GESTURES

Now that we've cataloged the five fingers on your hand, we can turn to the application of those fingers for gesturing. At the Hand & Knuckle Society we believe in clarity of communication, but, as you'll see, a gesture can mean many things. So read up to begin gesticulating like a boss.

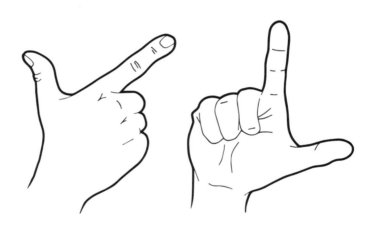

═══ INDEX AND THUMB ═══

aka: the finger gun, big L, the big pincher

Things it could mean:

☞ Loser.

☞ No good / nada.

☞ Right back at ya.

☞ Turn left.

☞ Two drinks.

☞ Hey, good lookin'. (accompanied by a wink)

☞ Whatever. (with both hands, the "Double Loser")

BEHIND THE FINGER GUN

Like a real firearm, the finger gun comes with great responsibility. It can be used to intimidate, add an exclamation to a three-point buzzer beater, or indicate *put me out of my misery*. And, as a greeting, it can "shoot" good vibes at your target. Unfortunately, coworkers and uncles everywhere have overused this variation for generations. But we believe it's possible to restore this gesture to its rightful esteemed position with the following rules.

DO:

- ☞ Offer gun between chest and eye level for optimum spotting.
- ☞ Keep thumb upright at all times.
- ☞ Add a single wink when you pull the trigger to make it more affectionate, less like target practice.
- ☞ Stagger double guns with one hand forward and one aligned behind it.

DON'T:

- ☞ Blow fake smoke from the index finger.
- ☞ Place in imaginary holster on your waist.
- ☞ Aim in the direction of a police officer.

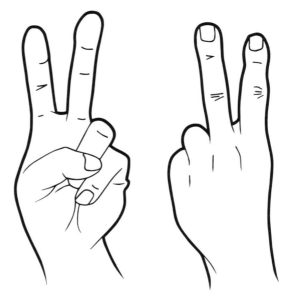

INDEX AND MIDDLE FINGER

aka: the peace sign, the Dick Nixon, the ol' one-two

Things it could mean:

- ☞ Peace.
- ☞ Peace out.
- ☞ Victory!
- ☞ Girl power! (as a Spice Girl)

- ☞ We're number 2!
- ☞ Table for two.
- ☞ [Bunny ears]

GLOBAL WARNING: THE PEACE SIGN

When performing a peace or victory sign in Australia, it's imperative you keep your palm facing out. If your palm faces inward, it's a vulgar insult—as evidenced by former president George H. W. Bush's unfortunate mishap in 1992, which left the Aussies no choice but to respond in kind.

INDEX AND PINKY

aka: ends up, hand horn, corna

Things it could mean:

- ☞ Rock on!
- ☞ Bull.
- ☞ Hook 'em horns! (at a Texas Longhorns game)
- ☞ [Protection from evil eye] (when pointed down)
- ☞ [Italian curse] (when pointed at someone)
- ☞ You're a cuckold.
- ☞ [Devil horns]

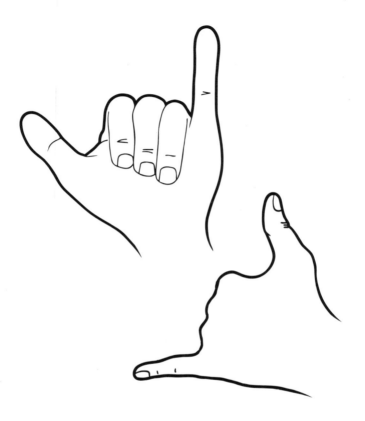

THUMB AND PINKY
aka: the faux phone, the span, the drinkie drinkie, the biggie small

Things it could mean:

☞ Call me! (when facing up)

☞ Hang up the phone. (when facing down)

☞ Wanna grab a drink?

☞ You must be drinking.

☞ Hang loose! (aka the shaka)

BEHIND THE SHAKA

"Shaka, brah!" This is a common greeting among surfers across the world, said while extending the popular Hawaiian "shaka" hand gesture. The gesture—performed by sticking out one's pinky and thumb while folding the three middle fingers down and twisting the hand side to side—is used to convey a number of things, such as friendship, unity, and welcome.

Originally, the shaka had one main meaning, which it still carries today: "Hang loose!" The symbol and term was first adopted by surfers, which makes sense considering that many believe it was originally used to represent the life cycle of an ocean wave, rising high with the pinky finger, slowly curling down with the middle fingers and flowing out into a smooth tide with the thumb.

While surfers around the world adopted the shaka and made it famous, it's not completely clear where the popular Hawaiian gesture comes from, as nothing like it exists in Polynesian culture. One popular legend suggests the shaka can be traced to a man named Hamana Kalili, who lost his middle three fingers working in a sugar mill in the early 20th century. After losing his digits Kalili worked security on a freight train frequented by kid surfers who sneaked on the trail to get to Sunset Beach. Kalili would often wave these kids away by raising his two-fingered hand—thus, the kids would mimic the gesture as a way to let one another know when Kalili wasn't around to stop their surfing trips.

Regardless of its origins, beach dwellers and mainlanders alike still commonly use the shaka to wish peace upon others.

THUMB, INDEX FINGER, AND PINKY

aka: three the hard way, the Gene Simmons

Things it could mean:

☞ ILY. ("I love you")

☞ Rock on! (variation)

☞ [Devil horns] (variation)

☞ [Shooting a web] (if Spider-Man)

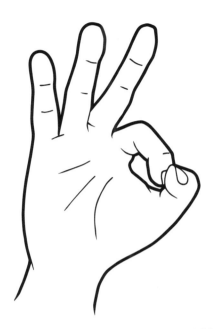

MIDDLE, RING, AND PINKY FINGERS

aka: the okay, the okey-dokey, the perfecto, the kind neighbor

Things it could mean:

- ☞ I'm okay!
- ☞ Perfect!
- ☞ Three of those things are left.
- ☞ Yes, that is correct.
- ☞ Very good.

GLOBAL WARNING: BRAZIL BEWARE

The "Okay Sign" is considered obscene in Brazil. So don't do it, okay? Okay.

THE FIST

*aka: knuckle sandwich, the enforcer, the widow maker,
the portable door knocker, five-knuckle value pack*

Things it could mean:

-  Fight the power!
- Right on!
- Go get 'em, Tiger!
- I would like to engage in fisticuffs.

- To the moon!
- Strike! (in baseball)
- F-yeah! (at a concert)

THE FIG SIGN

aka: the peeping turtle, mano fico, *"Say 'hello' to my little thumb,"* manus obscena

Things it could mean:

☞ I've got your nose.
☞ I'm protecting myself against the evil eye.
☞ [Intercourse]
☞ [Lady parts]

GLOBAL WARNING: THE FIG SIGN

Around the world—in Indonesia, Japan, Korea, Russia, Serbia, and Turkey—this twist on the fist is an obscene gesture. It is said that it looks like a sexual act, which might explain why some report that the ancient Greeks used it as a sign of fertility and good luck.

OH, SNAP! WE ALMOST FORGOT SNAPS!

Finger snaps are a great form of communication that can be used for a variety of purposes like helping to get someone's attention, keeping rhythm to music, applauding (for beatniks), or getting someone to literally snap out of it. The practice was raised to an expressive art form in the 1990s by characters from TV's *In Living Color* who incorporated nuanced variations and combinations including double snaps and triple snaps (in a Z formation).

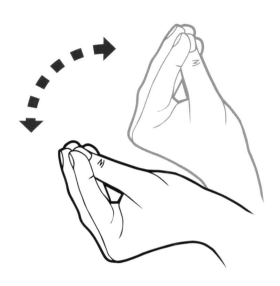

THE MANO A BORSA

aka: purse in hand, the scoop, the punctuation mark

Things it could mean:

☞ What are you doing?

☞ WTF?

☞ This is a very important (but perhaps unanswerable) question.

'SUP WITH MANO A BORSA?

This gesture translates to "purse in hand," and is seen in everyday Italian life. It is used to accentuate a question or can be used without words as a way to simply say, "What do you want from me?"

MAKE WAVES

While waving is used around the world as a greeting, the way you wave makes a big difference. Here are five different waves to consider.

1. Jazz Hands Wave

Also known as the "Look, Mom, I'm on TV" wave, it is similar to a basic garden-variety wave but with an extra dose of fabulousness: both hands are employed. Double the fingers, double the fun.

2. Royal Wave

The hand is rigid, cupped slightly, and held high as the wrist twists slightly back and forth. It's executed perfectly by members of the royal family as a sign of their class and stiff upper lips.

3. Pageant Wave

Similar to the Royal Wave. Bring the middle finger slightly toward the thumb and instead of just a wrist twist, the forearm also moves in a "wash the windows" motion. Metaphorically, of course—a beauty queen would never do windows.

4. Driving Wave

This driving gesture is a slow, broad wave with an open palm that says, "Thanks for letting me merge into the lane."

5. The Faraway Wave

There's no better way of getting someone to stand up and take notice than by resorting to this wave. A popular greeting among castaways and the overly caffeinated, this full-body greeting requires you to jump up and down while flapping your arm back and forth above your head.

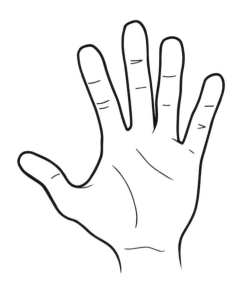

ALL FIVE DIGITS

aka: the full house, the open palm, the full spread

Things it could mean if extended:

☞ Talk to the hand.

☞ Wait.

☞ Stop!

☞ I'll take five of those things.

☞ Hi!

GLOBAL WARNING: IT'S ALL GREEK TO ME

In Greece, raising all five fingers is a traditional insult called the "moutza." The closer the palm is to the victims face, the more insulting it is—like an extreme version of "talk to the hand!"

AIR QUOTE VS. AIR HASHTAG: 2 HANDS, 2 FINGERS, 2 SIGNALS

When trying to add "irony" or emphasize #keywords while talking, the air quote or air hashtag can help "accentuate" and better articulate your #trueintentions—without having to actually say "quote" or "hashtag." Here are the key differences between these "gestures" or #gestures.

Air Quote
- ☞ Quoting someone else
- ☞ Sarcastic
- ☞ Euphemistic
- ☞ Analog
- ☞ Chris Farley

Air Hashtag
- ☞ Making up a phrase
- ☞ Ironic
- ☞ Literal
- ☞ Digital
- ☞ Jimmy Fallon

THE RIGHT-HAND PATH

As you're high-fiving, handshaking, and fist-bumping your way through the rest of this book, you're likely to notice a common theme: many hand gestures and greetings are exclusively performed by the right hand (except for those notoriously rebellious Boy Scouts). Not only is the right hand the preferred hand, it's also the proper hand. In other words, greeting with the left hand can be seen as impolite by some and downright disgusting by others.

So why is this? What makes ol' lefty the Fredo to the righty's Michael Corleone?

To answer that in a word: Satan.

While some cultures, particularly those in the Middle East, consider the left hand a dirty tool reserved for cleaning armpits and other less savory places, many other cultures associate the left hand with the Devil himself. This is because Satan is possibly the world's first lefty; numerous tales, paintings, and portrayals depict the Prince of Darkness always using his left hand. Because of this, the left hand has often been (perhaps unfairly) associated with the Devil and his dark ways. It's no wonder we have so many superstitions and sayings that revolve around the "left-hand path"—because anything done on the lefty is bound to bring you bad luck courtesy of Beelzebub himself.

Moral of the story: always greet with the right hand—it's what's expected, what's common knowledge, and just the way it is and almost always has been. So deal with it unless you want to embrace the cold darkness of the Devil himself, which is typically considered a faux pas unless you're in a metal band.

HIGH FIVE COMMANDMENT NO. 2
"TRUTH IS REVEALED NOT BY WORDS BUT THROUGH GESTURE."

CHAPTER 2

CIVILITIES & SHAKES

Aficionados and connoisseurs all celebrate their classics. For wine lovers, it might be a Côte de Nuits. For car collectors, it might be a Pininfarina Ferrari. For 1980s sitcom fans, it might be season one of *Small Wonder*.

For the Hand & Knuckle Society, it's another set of classics that we reserve for the finer moments in life. For centuries, classics like bows, curtsies, handshakes, and salutes have set the standards for greetings. While the high five is often the epitome of hand gestures, some may find it simply too awesome for life's more formal situations, such as job interviews, military functions, and meeting your date's judgmental father. For such occasions, we tap the wisdom of some more time-honored signs of respect.

This chapter is dedicated to mastering these timeless greetings—a class in the classics, a schooling in the old-school, a firm grasp of firm grasps.

THE BOW

Simultaneously a sign of a true gentleman and the mark of a humble warrior, the bow is typically performed by hinging your body at the hips as a way to lower your head (and, more symbolically, your very existence) below that of someone else. The act of bowing is an enduring display of one's deep respect, and shows a commendable amount of lower back flexibility.

HOW IT STARTED

Another fellow esoteric society, the Wu Tang Clan, urges everyone to "Protect Ya Neck." But a bow goes against the Wu. When a person bows, he's taking his eyes off the other person as well as exposing his head and neck, two of the most vulnerable spots on the body. By opting not to protect one's neck, the bower demonstrates complete trust and says, "I respect you enough to give you a cheap shot, but I trust you not to take it."

HOW TO DO IT

Bow down to the bow. This respectful genuflection will serve you well when you've just encountered any of the following: a standing ovation, the entrance shrine at your dojo, the sign-in sheet at a yoga class, or time travel to the Victorian era. The bow has many cultural and contextual variations, but the main move remains the same: bend from the waist—not the neck. (That's a nod.)

Bring Your Shoulders Up Begin by standing straight up with your feet close together and your hands hanging at your sides. Stand with your shoulders squared and facing your target.

 Offer Your Gaze Downward Relax your neck and lower your head as if dropping your chin to the chest.

 Waist, Bend at It Begin bending at the waist, keeping your back straight and hinging your upper body downward. The lower you bend, the more respect you give.

TYPES OF BOWS

Bows are a lot like deities—every culture has them, and they always seem weird unless they're the ones you recognize. Here are some of the most widely known and exercised.

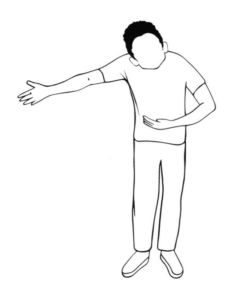

THE CLASSIC BOW

aka: the butler bow, the prim & proper, the Downton Abbey

The Classic Bow is one of the most common forms of bowing on the Western side of the world. A sign of proper etiquette, the Classic is a classy way to greet and welcome someone of authority.

NAMASTE

aka: the Indian spiritual bow, the Whole Foods greeting

As its namesake suggests, this mindful move originated in India.
Often linked to certain Eastern spiritual practices and
ponytailed vegan yoga instructors, the Namaste involves
pressing both palms together so the fingers point to the sky as
you dip into a slight bend. Om.

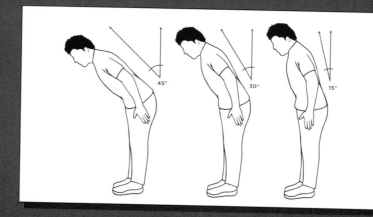

THE JAPANESE BOW

To the Japanese, bowing is practically a second language, and an intricate one at that. There are different types of bows and styles that are used on a regular basis—ranging from standing to kneeling—and for various occasions, such as religious functions, sporting events, classroom settings, and work situations. Bowing can also be a display of an abstract concept, such as showing respect, remorse, humility, and submission.

There are also precise variations for bows that differ based on certain situations. For instance, the timing of a bow depends on the person to whom you're bowing. If you're bowing to a superior, such as your boss, you'll not only bow your head lower than she does, but you'll stay bowed down longer.

Bowing is such a big deal that the Japanese continue to do it in addition to adopting gestures from other cultures. It's not uncommon to see a handshake accompanied by a bow. Or even long-distance bowing to each other, while talking on the phone.

KARATE BOW

aka: the dojo bow, the domo arigato, *the Ralph Macchio, the ka-ra-taaay*

Most martial arts disciplines use some form of bowing, typically to show respect to teachers, peers, and opponents. Aside from showing respect, bows are also used to signify that you're about to crane-kick a sucker in the face!

STAGE BOW

aka: the Shakespeare dip, the leg-breaker, the bow diddley

Associated with the bright lights and floppy wigs of the theater, this communal bow comes at the end of the show when all the major players in the production take the stage, hold hands, and bow while the audience throws kisses, roses, and/or underwear.

HOW NOW KOWTOW?

The elaborate Chinese bowing ritual known as kowtowing (literally, "head knocking") involves dropping to one's knees, bending forward until one's head touches the ground, raising the head, and touching the ground again, then repeating the process once more before standing back up. Then the CrossFit-worthy process is repeated twice more. The kowtow has largely been replaced by the more traditional bow. And the term "kowtow" is now used in English to describe excessive butt-kissing behavior.

THE CURTSY

Back in the day, some considered bowing to be unladylike. That's where the curtsy came in. Taking the bow and making it decidedly more feminine, the curtsy was created not only for showing respect, but also for receiving it. So, when a gentleman would bow to a lady, it was common etiquette to curtsy back.

HOW IT STARTED

The word "curtsy" actually derives from the word "courtesy," which makes sense considering it was intended as a polite gesture. As legend has it, the gesture symbolized an inferiority or deference to the males and/or the royalty for whom it was being performed. As times changed and greetings became less formalized, the curtsy went the way of the Black Plague—known well by reputation, though rarely seen in modern times. That said, it's always good to keep your curtsy game strong.

HOW TO DO IT

What do dance recitals, debutante balls, and royal courts have in common? All are places where you're bound to witness a curtsy. Some require a little bend in the knees, while others get low, low, low—so go ahead and get down.

Close Your Eyes and Bow Your Head With eyes closed, nod your head downward and smile politely. Get comfortable: your head is going to be in this position for the entire gesture.

 Uphold Your Posture Grab the sides of your dress. Now, raise your arms up to the sides so the fabric creates a fan-like shape. If you're not in a frock, pretend you are and mime the motions.

 Reach Your Foot Out Extend your right foot and plant it in front of you. Place your left foot perpendicular to it so the right foot almost meets the big toe of the left foot to form an "L" shape.

 Tilt at the Knees Keeping your feet planted, bend both knees outward. As your knees bend outward, keep your back straight and resist the urge to bend at the waist. Try not to fall over.

 Straighten Back Up Slowly elevate yourself back up to the starting position. As you rise, uncross your feet, let go of your dress, and un-bow your head.

 Yeah, You Just Curtsied That's right. You just performed the classic classy move. Time to revel in your own elegance.

TYPES OF CURTSIES

Curtsying may be uncommon in daily life, but should you marry into royalty, become a diplomat, or join a Shakespeare troupe, you'll be doing it constantly. A note on form: as with athletic squats, try to keep your knees from extending past your toes, especially if you've got bad knees and/or high heels on.

THE SIMPLE CURTSY
aka: the courteous curtsy, the lady bow

As simple as it is elegant, the Simple Curtsy has a bit of an all-purpose function. Seen most often when introducing oneself or responding to a gentleman's bow, the Simple Curtsy is one of the most ladylike ways to say, "What 'tis upeth with thou?"

THE COURT CURTSY

aka: the royal dip, the God Save the Queen

As the name suggests, the Court Curtsy was once reserved as a
sign of respect for members of the high-and-mighty monarchies
in Europe. This curtsy is performed like the Simple Curtsy,
but requires getting much lower, deeper, and snootier.

THE BALLET CURTSY

*aka: the pointe curtsy,
the bravo-bravo bend, the dancer's dip*

The Ballet Curtsy originates from—you guessed it—the ballet. More
specifically, the ballerina uses it after a performance to thank not
only the audience, but also the musicians, directors, and stagehands.
Donning a painfully tight bun and austere gaze is purely optional.

THE TEXAS DIP
aka: the debutante duck, the southern belle, the dip-a-dee-doo-dah

Never one to be messed with, this big curtsy is performed by Texan debutantes and involves extending your arms to the side and lowering so low that one physically becomes a part of the Deep South.

THE NOD

Greetings and congratulatory gestures can get pretty elaborate, but some-times you just want to say "hi" without moving, standing, or even opening your mouth. This is why the nod remains one of the easiest and best ways to greet someone as well as show your approval of their actions and presence. The gesture consists of bobbing one's head up and down (or down and up). Though the gesture is simple, no two ways of nodding your head mean the same thing.

HOW IT STARTED

Some believe that nodding branched out from bowing, with the nod being a sort of shorthand version used to show agreement and acceptance from a superior party. Others, though, have noted that infant children, when hungry, tend to nod upwards while looking for and accepting food (and, interestingly enough, shake their heads from left to right when denying it), suggesting that the nod is a natural evolution that comes from this ingrained, accepting behavior.

HOW TO DO IT

Acknowledgment, thy name is nod. Understatement, simplicity, and a slight air of detachment combine in this powerful move. Detractors may argue that it's lazy, but practitioners know that its silence is its strength. Just nod if you agree.

N Neutral Gaze   Nodding is a reactionary gesture often triggered by an outside influence such as a question or a greeting. Because of this, the first step in nodding is to not nod at all. Keep your neck and head relaxed and eyes facing forward and ready to respond.

O Observe the Recipient   Once the impetus for a nod has been revealed (fancy talk for "nudging the nod"), face your target and make eye contact. Otherwise, the recipient may not know you're nodding and may just assume you have a nervous twitch.

D Dip and Bob   With eye contact established, initiate the nod by lowering your chin slightly downward toward your chest. Keep the chin in that downward position for a brief second, then bob it back up. Maintain eye contact and bask in the glow of unspoken cool.

TYPES OF NODS

Simple as they may be, nods can come in a number of different forms to convey a number of meanings. Use these variations to help pack a lot of meaning in a little bit of motion.

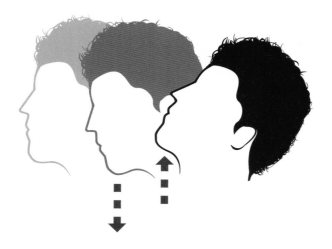

THE CLASSIC NOD
aka: the bob, the basic bob, the chin dip

**The nod that started it all. A simple drop of the chin
while maintaining eye contact is all you need
to say hello, show agreement, exhibit pride, and do just about
anything else. It's like the Leatherman tool of gestures.**

THE 'SUP NOD

aka: the bro nod, the what-up, the hey man, the duuude

Popular in the "bro" community, this nod starts down low with
the chin toward the chest and explodes upward, practically
screaming "Yo!" to anyone in its crosshairs. The go-to nod for
communicating on a bro-tastic level or for inspiring a bro-mance.

THINGS YOU CAN SAY WITH A NOD

☞ Mhmm.
☞ Good day, kind sir.
☞ Whassup?

☞ Yup!
☞ Oh, hells yeah!

THE POWER NOD
aka: the machismo, el jefe, the O Captain! My Captain!

A favorite of coaches, military leaders, and martial arts senseis,
the Power Nod is often used by superiors to show approval
and pride to their charges. Starting with the eyes
and staring straight forward, this nod is done with a single,
exaggerated up-to-down motion.

THE EYEBROW FLASH
aka: the brow wave, the hi-brow

Considered to be one the most universal of greetings,
it appears in cultures around the world, and even within
communities of monkeys. The simple raising of one's eyebrows
is quickly understood to mean, "Hey there, how are you doing?
Let's be civil and not throw feces at each other. Eek, eek."

THE GOOD DAY
aka: the London dandy, the tally ho, the yes siree Bob

A more chipper variation of the Classic Nod, the Good Day is said
to have originated in Victorian England when men were gentleman
and top hats didn't seem silly. This move functions similarly to the
Classic Nod; however, it's enhanced by the nodder adding a hand
to the brim of his hat while smiling and saying, "Good day!"

THE HASSLE OF THE HAT DOFF

The Hat Doff is a combination of the nod and the hat tip with a touch of charm thrown in for good measure. While (sadly) not a commonly used term, "doff" is the opposite of "don" and means to remove. So while removing your hat to show respect sounds straightforward, it isn't—or at least it wasn't from the 16th to the 18th centuries in England. During this hat-doffing heyday, it was a big, elaborate, complex deal. A complicated set of etiquette rules governed who, when, and even how much height each person required in the hat-raising-and-lowering department. Thankfully dress codes became more casual, culture became a bit more relaxed, and hat doffing was, well, doffed.

THE SALUTE

The salute is a greeting with the potential to be as badass as the soldiers who most commonly use it. Versatile in nature, salutes aren't limited to one general motion but typically combine hand motions and other gestures and slogans as well.

HOW IT STARTED

Salutes are most commonly tied to certain groups and subsets, such as military branches or religious sects. In a lot of ways, the salute almost functions as a sort of secret handshake—it's typically used to show others, "Hey, I'm not only one of you, but I respect the heck out of you, too!" The reasons for saluting may be clear, but the origins? Not so much.

In Western cultures, it's said that the salute began back in the Middle Ages when armored knights would lift the visors on their helmets to not only make friendly eye contact, but to symbolically say, "I'm showing my face to you, as I'm not afraid of you." The salute, however, didn't turn into a sign of respect until more modern times, according to the US Quartermaster Center and School. As visors evolved into harder-to-remove gear, saluting was shortened to more of a hand-to-the-brow motion.

HOW TO DO IT

All hail the salute, a soldierly greeting with civilian variations. Most salutes, whether performed by lovers or fighters, have specific rules regarding their use. In short, you don't need to bear arms for these militaristic motions—just arms.

Straighten It Up Salutes are a sign of respect, which is pretty difficult to show if you're slouching. Start by standing up straight and keeping your feet together.

 Angle It Up Raise your right hand to your head in a quick snapping motion.

 Level It Out Your upper arm should be parallel to the ground at all times.

 Upright Your elbow should be bent at a 45-degree angle while your forearm, wrist, and hand are all aligned in a rigid straight line. Neither the palm nor the back of the hand should be visible.

 Touch Your right index finger should be lightly touching your eyebrow or visor (if you're wearing a hat).

 End It Hold this position until a salute is returned, then snap your hand quickly back to normal position. At ease, soldier, at ease.

TYPES OF SALUTES

The interesting thing about salutes is that they aren't all just formality and flying arms. Here are some of history's favorite salutes.

TWO-FINGER SALUTE
aka: the scout's honor, the dynamic duo, the two direction

A favorite of Cub Scouts and the "bad boy" member of boy bands alike, the two-finger salute follows a process similar to the military salute. However, it requires the user to keep only the middle and index finger extended while the other three fold down.

GLADIATOR SALUTE

*aka: the salute that never was, the fight-
the-power fist, the Caesar salute*

Ave Imperator, morituri te salutant (Hail, Emperor, those who are about
to die salute you!) is said to be the salute gladiators would yell before
battling to the death for the emperor's amusement. Today, it's said before
less dire situations, like football games and beer pong tournaments.

BEHIND THE MILITARY SALUTE

In the US military, the salute is an extension of the discipline and respect that's instilled into military personnel from the first day of basic training. In fact, according to veteran Corporal Jason Walker of the United States Marine Corps 2nd and 3rd Recon Battalions, saluting properly is so important to military practice, it's emphasized just as much as any other soldier skill.

"Failure to render a proper salute would often result in a less-than-desirable outcome for us," remembers Walker. "Besides the psychological beating from drill instructors yelling in your face, push-ups, flutter kicks, and eight-count body builders were kindly offered for failing to properly salute."

So what counts as a proper salute? Here's Walker's advice on how to avoid making the real US military weep:

Don't Salute … ?: It's actually forbidden to salute while wearing civilian attire or while in combat. Saluting a member of the military if you're a civilian is even worse.

Don't Leave Anyone Out: All US officers, officers of allied countries, the President of the United States, and recipients of the Medal of Honor require salutes from enlisted personnel.

Don't Use Your Left Hand: Saluting comes from soldiers raising their empty right (or "weapon") hand as a sign of peace, which is why using ol' lefty to salute can lead to plenty o' push-ups.

Don't Forget the Tunes: There are also songs that all US military person-nel are required to salute, including "The Star Spangled Banner," "Hail to the Chief," "To the Color," or any foreign national anthem.

Don't Salute When Holding Something: This is a mistake President Barack Obama infamously made when trying to salute while holding coffee. "If he wasn't the president he would be doing push-ups and flutter kicks all day long," says Walker.

VULCAN SALUTE

aka: the Starship salute, the L.L.A.P., that thing Spock does

Most famously performed by Spock on *Star Trek*, the Vulcan Salute involves raising your right hand and forming a "V" by spreading your middle and ring fingers apart. While flashing this sign, complete the salute by declaring, "Live long and prosper" to the recipient, a sign of good tidings on an intergalactic level.

ZOGIST SALUTE

*aka: the chest chopper, the Albanian
acknowledgment, the Zoggy Stardust*

Often confused with the you-must-be-this-tall-to-ride gesture,
the Zogist salute is performed by placing your right hand over
your heart with your palm facing the floor. The salute was
originally created by Albanian king Zog I as a means of military
salute. Today it's used by the military and citizens of Albania—
as well as the Hand & Knuckle Society members, of course.

THE HANDSHAKE

Few things are as universal as the handshake. One person extends his or her hand out to another person. The other person returns the gesture, accepting the first person's hand. The hands join and wrap around each other to literally shake for a few short moments before letting go. Just like the ending of *Titanic*, everyone knows how handshakes go. Unlike *Titanic*, though, there should be a lot less crying at the end.

HOW IT STARTED

The handshake was most likely invented sometime in 5th century BC Greece as a symbol to suggest "hands hold no weapons." In Rome, this gesture continued as a symbol of peace showing that neither person was armed, which is why the original version involved grabbing each other's forearm (vs. the hand), just in case you needed to make sure your chum wasn't stashing a knife up his sleeve.

In the middle ages, the handshake evolved to a gripping of the hands to shake loose any weapons that may have been concealed. While the actual act of handshaking got a little smaller, paranoia did not. Fortunately, much of the backstabbing done in modern times is usually executed with words instead of knives, making the handshake a much safer and more enjoyable gesture than it once was.

HOW TO DO IT

The classic handshake has its fans in movers, shakers, dealmakers, and regular folk who just want to say, "Pleased to meet you." Riffs on it are ever-evolving, so just remember to keep it firm, not floppy. Should we shake on it?

Share Eye Contact Direct eye contact is the cornerstone of a great handshake. Begin by approaching the recipient and allowing your eyes to meet and lock.

 Hand Over Your Hand Initiate the handshake by raising your right hand up to about belly button height and extending it to the recipient.

 Accept Their Hand As the hands meet, grip the other person's hand so that the webbing between your thumb and forefinger presses against the webbing of their hand.

 Keep and Pump With both hands joined, pump the hands in an up-and-down motion one to three times and then release.

 Early Release It's important to release the hand shortly after the third pump. Better to release the grip early than hold on too long, as the latter implies you have something more to say—or that you're desperate for human touch.

TYPES OF HANDSHAKES

There are going to be times in life when you'll need to up your hand-on-hand game. Pull these variations out of your sleeve to bring your handshakes to the next level.

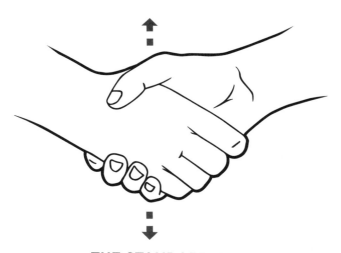

THE STANDARD GRIP

aka: the old fashioned, the gentleman's grip

Efficient and elegant, the Standard Grip handshake is still one of the easiest ways to show off your manners. As classic as apple pie and just as warm, the Standard Grip is always best-in-class when it comes to handshakes.

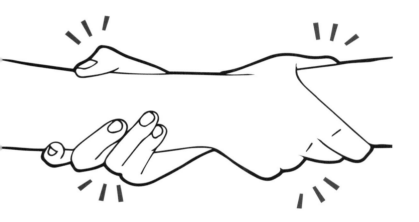

THE FOREARM GRIP

aka: the gladiator grip, the Maximus, the man clutch

Spartan in look and Herculean in scope, few handshakes express
manliness like the Forearm Grip. In this original version of the
handshake, participants reach out to one another as they normally
would, but instead of joining hands both people reach past the
wrists and wrap their hand around the other person's forearm.

THE DOUBLE-HANDED POLITICIAN
aka: the double fister, the presidential, the I'm-down-with-the-people shake

For the candidate who wants to show he cares more than his opponent, the Double-Handed Politician uses a rapid single-pump shake with both hands simultaneously in order to press the flesh with twice as many hands in half the time.

HANDSHAKE DO'S AND DON'TS

Simple as they may be, handshakes present a minefield of social faux pas to avoid. Proper etiquette can add a serious level of seriousness to your shake.

DO:

Have clean, dry hands: We shouldn't have to say this, and neither should the person receiving your damp digits.

Be firm: Know what kind of person shakes with a limp hand? We don't, because we don't want to meet that person and neither does anybody else.

Know who initiates: The person with home-field advantage should always initiate (e.g., if someone comes to your office, you initiate).

Stand up: You should never take a handshake sitting down.

DON'T:

Wipe your hand on your pants: Try to get the cleaning/drying process handled prior to the exchange if possible.

Extend from too far away: Wait until you're close enough to touch before offering it up.

Extend from too close: Give just enough personal space—not too much, not too little.

Linger: Go in, grasp, make one or two pumps, and then let it go. Anything more is . . . well, kind of weird.

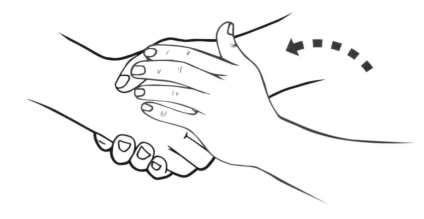

THE SHAKE AND COVER

*aka: the glove grip, the there-there, the
I feel you, the silent threat*

This gesture takes the standard handshake and covers both your hand
and the other person's, as if protecting the hands from rain. It's typically
saved for more solemn occasions, such as greeting someone in mourning
or when making serious threats to a sworn enemy face-to-face.

EXTRA HAND ENHANCERS

The left hand can be like a punctuation mark to
the right hand's shake. Here are several escalating
positions and what they might communicate.

1. *Back of right hand: "I'm so sorry."*
2. *Wrist: "Thank you so much."*
3. *Elbow: "Honored to meet you."*
4. *Bicep: "Wow. I didn't think you had it in you."*
5. *Back of neck: "Don't let me catch you doing that again."*

THE SELF-SHAKE

*aka: we're-in-this-together clasp, the pump
up the jam, the clasping at straws*

This is a symbolic gesture that allows the shaker to virtually shake
with a crowd. Used by triumphant athletes and politicians alike,
the self-shake is usually performed about the shoulders
with slight pumps to either side.

THINGS YOU SHOULD SAY TO GET A HANDSHAKE

While you can likely get away with offering a simple "Hello," true
handshake mastery involves connecting with the mind as well as
the palm. Here are a few lines to drop as you go hand-in-hand:

☞ *Put 'er there!*
☞ *Let's shake on it.*
☞ *Let's press the flesh.*

☞ *Darn glad to meet ya!*
☞ *My handshake brings all
the boys to the yard.*

HANDSHAKE PRANKS

This list of flourishes gives the standard handshake an extra message.

1. The Joy Buzzer

What to Do: Place a small mechanized device on your hand to deliver a harmless shock to any hand you shake.

What It Says: You want a good laugh, even at the considerable expense of another's dignity.

2. The Finger Tickle

What to Do: While in mid-handshake, curl your fingers in and caress the other person's palm.

What It Says: You're a little flirty. And you're totally okay with making the other person extremely uncomfortable.

3. The Bone Crusher

What to Do: Squeeze the ever-lovin' mercy out of the other person's hand as a show of aggression and dominance.

What It Says: You're more than willing to decimate another human being's precious digits—or are a father being forced to shake hands with your daughter's boyfriend.

4. The Knuckle Roll

What to Do: Create an undulating motion with the shakee's knuckles. Not painful enough to bring tears, but almost.

What It Says: You're that guy. Don't be that guy.

THE FOUR-FINGER CLASP
aka: the limp wrist, the weak welcome
wagon, the delicate flower

Not quite a real handshake, the four-finger clasp is done by offering
your four fingers to the recipient with the expectation that they'll
grab only those fingers for a shake. Dainty in nature, this "handshake"
is referred to as a "girly" handshake, likely because it's the go-to
for old ladies who are still expecting you to kiss their hand.

THE WINNING-A-GIANT-CHECK SHAKE
aka: the diploma shake, the photo-op shake, the jackpot

Special occasions require a special handshake, and what occasion is
more special than the day you finally receive that massive check from
Publishers Clearing House? This involves accepting your giant honor in
one hand while shaking the hand of your benefactor with the other—
all while facing the camera and flashing a grin bigger than the check.

THE HAND-OFF HANDSHAKE
aka: the shakedown shake, the VIP
(Very Important Payment), the Chicago shake

This is a shake with a surprise where the shaker discreetly holds
an object, usually folded cash, under his or her thumb and passes
it to the shakee's palm during the act of the handshake. Best used
when bribing a bouncer or hostess at a happening spot.

HOW TO CREATE YOUR OWN SECRET HANDSHAKE

Shrouded in mystery and cast in shadows, secret handshakes have been a staple of underground organizations for thousands of years. Powerful groups like the Freemasons, Skull and Bones, and the Goonies have all been rumored to use secret handshakes to identify members and protect themselves against curious outsiders. The intricacy of the exchange varies from group to group. In some cases secret handshakes can also involve the touching of feet, elbows, or even the lips.

These days, secret handshakes live on in the rituals—and between the beer pong games—of fraternities and sororities across America.

Other secret greetings are not-so-secretive, like the Boy Scouts, who openly use their left-handed shake with other members in public.

Of course, we know a thing or two about secret organizations and secret shakes. But maybe we've already said too much.

Create Your Own Secret Handshake

We can't tell you our secret shake so the next best thing is to create your own. But first you need a few people, a secret mission, and a hidden location for meetings (a tree house will do for anyone under twelve).

Step 1: Pick an Initiation

Every secret handshake has to start somewhere, right? The initiation shows the recipient you're a member of his or her super-secret crew and you're ready to throw down some secret salutes.

Examples include:

- ☞ A double-tap on the nose
- ☞ A tricky blinking pattern
- ☞ A password

Step 2: Select a Shake

The meat of your secret handshake doesn't necessarily have to be a hand-shake, per se. As long as you've got a gesture of camaraderie in there, you should be all good.

Examples include:

- ☞ Bashing of forearms
- ☞ A high five
- ☞ A fist bump

Step 3: Finish with a Flourish

This is the time to get imaginative, and to let your freak flag fly—secretly, of course. The finisher is the defining moment of the secret handshake, the part that ties it all together—the secret sauce of the secret shakes, if you will.

Examples include:

- ☞ A snap and a clap
- ☞ A double chest bump
- ☞ A pinky pop and lock

HIGH FIVE COMMANDMENT NO. 3
"HONOUR THY FRIENDS WITH SIGNS ONLY OF RESPECT."

CHAPTER 3

HUGS & KISSES

It's time we all expanded our repertoire of respect, our palette of politeness, and our fanny pack of friendliness. It's time for some touchy and some feely. That's right, it's time for hugs and kisses.

Hugs and kisses are natural behaviors in a romantic context, and as evidenced by public displays of affection, they can happen anywhere. But take love and lust out of the equation, and you have two highly charged greetings—greetings that have protocols and rules to keep platonic parties from becoming, as experts say, all up in each other's business.

Nothing beats reconnecting with a solid hug from an old friend. But when awkwardness prevails, these potent greetings can be quite painful, too. Few things are as unforgettable as the social shame of bungling a cheek kiss with your boss's wife.

All of this makes hugs and kisses high-touch as well as high stress. For these reasons, we present to you the ABCs of the X's and O's.

HUGS

Call it an embrace, a squeeze, a clutch. The non-romantic hug is possibly the most universal salutation of all. Sure, the high five is still the most awesome, but the hug could be the most significant. In today's disconnected world, human connection has become more important than ever. There is just something about the deliberate and mutual breaking of our personal boundaries that makes us feel truly welcome.

HOW IT STARTED

The hug is hardwired into our DNA—as natural a sign of affection as you can find. Kids do it. Primates do it. (Birds and bees don't have arms, but they'd do it if they could.) It's one of those instinctive acts that we use to express love, care, comfort, friendship, and warm-fuzziness.

HOW TO DO IT

Embrace the possibility that lies within the hug. A hug can be "hello," but it can also be "goodbye." Those open arms can convey support or sympathy—or enthusiasm and excitement. This multipurpose show of affection can be used almost anywhere, except perhaps the workplace. Unless, of course, your job is delivering winning lottery checks.

C Communicate Before you hug, articulate your intentions. Some people say, "Let's hug it out," or "Gimme some of that yum-yum." Of course, feel free to use your own, non-creepy words.

O Open Spread your arms to signal that a hug is coming. Look for reciprocity. If you need to beckon with your hands, that can work fine, too.

M Move On In You can't hug outside of arm's length, so move into the recipient's personal space. Again, be sure to look for signs they are down to hug.

E Entry Getting the correct docking fit is crucial—so approach with your head tilted and your right arm slightly raised to telegraph the right position.

H Hit Gently bump upper torsos as you wrap your arms around their back. Apply pressure with both arms, but show restraint. A little squeeze goes a long way.

E Express Use your words. Verbally convey the reason for the hug. For example, "It was so good to see you," is acceptable. "Wow, this feels so good," is not.

R Release You must extricate after holding for the appropriate time. How long is that? Well, you just need to figure some things out for yourself.

E Exhale Wow, that really did feel good. Whew.

TYPES OF HUGS

Hugs offer plentiful opportunities for variation, and can be endlessly modified to fit any situation or relationship. Indeed, one advantage of the hug is that it can successfully convey intimacy without necessarily imparting it.

THE STANDARD HUG

aka: the A-frame, basic 'brace, the hugger's hug

This is a solid go-to hug: friendly and platonic, yet still warm-ish. The business end of this hug is in the shoulder area, where there is full contact. Everything from the chest down—especially the private stuff—is kept a safe distance apart.

THE BEAR HUG

aka: the bone crusher, the chiropractor crunch,
the Huggy Bear, the Lennie Small

Unlike the Standard Hug in which huggers alternate interlocking arms, the Bear Hugger places both arms around the huggee's chest and—this part is critical—lifts the huggee off the ground, squeezing the living crap out of him. Sort of like a reverse Heimlich maneuver.

THE OBLIGATORY HUG
aka: the awkward relative hug, the sucky squeeze, the ugh

**This technique is reserved for a hug full of reservations.
The patented butt-out/lean-in position allows for minimal
touching and maximum get-me-out-of-here.**

HUG LIFE

These are the top five ways a hug benefits your body and mind.

1. *Reduces stress*
2. *Lowers blood pressure*
3. *Boosts self-esteem*
4. *Increases oxytocin, a "bonding" hormone*
5. *Increases serotonin, a "happiness" hormone*

THE HALF HUG
aka: the single shoulder, the side hug, the friend-zoner

The name is accurate for this action. It's where the hugger and huggee only touch right shoulders and lightly embrace with their hands. It's a good option when time is limited, or when interest in hugging this person is also limited.

THE MIRACLE HUGS & CHOCOLATE LADY

Hugging strangers can be awkward, but that's never stopped the indomitable Mata Amritanandamayi, a spiritual leader who travels the world hugging people. Amma, as she's known informally, has embraced 34 million people (and counting). She's also been known to share kisses—the Hershey's kind.

THE FULL-HANDS HUG

aka: the I'm-holding-these-things hug; the shopper squash

Pop quiz: you have two piping hot eight-dollar double espressos in your hands and you run into a good (not great) friend. What do you do? Answer: the Full-Hands Hug! It shows you're attempting to be friendly but you have these things in your hands so, you know, this is all you're going to get.

HUGGING MISHAPS

A tender, warm embrace sounds good. But in reality, it takes a lot of nonverbal coordination and some plain old good luck to pull off a hug with ease.

The Side-to-Side Shuffle: This awkward gaffe happens when there is no clear decision on which side each party is going to assume. The result is a brief comedy of errors as the parties shuffle back and forth and flail their arms in an awkward two-step.

The Too-Long Hug: This hug overstays its welcome—and then some. When one party holds on for too long, it can quickly escalate from sweet and kind to kind of creepy in just over ten seconds.

The Too-Close Hug: Between two lovers, this is a passionate embrace that knows no bounds. Between two acquaintances, this is an embrace that crosses the line. Most hugs use the standard A-frame structure to keep pelvises apart. This one puts them (and the rest of the human anatomy) all up in each other's junk.

The Spill Hug: What happens when you have a drink in your hand—and several in your belly—and you hug someone at a party? In the Hand & Knuckle Society, we like to call it "giving someone the ol' liquid sweater." Not a good look, but a great Facebook post.

The Roving Hands: The difference between a greeting and a groping is the placement of the hands. As soon as they start to head south of the border, things become less touching and more touchy. Big difference.

THE HUG AND HOLD

aka: the look-at-you hug, the so good to see you, the ol' buddy, ol' pal

This is a build on the standard hug. After the initial embrace, the hugger remains connected, commonly either placing her hands on the huggee's shoulders and executing a double clasp grip. This allows time to reminisce about how much things haven't changed—or how much they have.

THE HIGH HUG

aka: the victory embrace, the heck-yeah hug, the woo-hoooo!

As the energy climbs, so do the arms of the hugger. A basic celebratory hug, the High Hug is similar to a Bear Hug but executed much higher up on the huggee's body. It screams, "I can't believe we won [the big championship/big sales pitch/big board game]!"

THE NOTEBOOK HUG

aka: the run 'n' hop hug, the lovers' lock, the full Gosling

This hug begins several yards back with a running start. It ends with bodies entangled and emotions off the charts. Of course, the raw spontaneity of the moment can be ruined if anyone has back problems and the hug becomes more of a flying tackle.

THE UNRECIPROCATED HUG
aka: the cold-shoulder hug, the corpse

This is not a hug one initiates, but instead a hug one receives. Rather than returning any friendly affection, the huggee just stands there, hands usually down to the side and eyes looking off to another place—a place they are imagining escaping to.

THE SORORITY FULL-BODY FREAK OUT
aka: the oh-em-gee!, the sisterhood squeeze, the BFFs 4eva embrace

This hug is a production. It starts several yards away when the hugger and huggee(s) notice each other. What follows is a series of screams, small running footsteps, more screams, flailing arms, OMG jazz hands, and more ear-splitting screams.

THE DRUNKEN HUG
aka: The I Love You, Man hug, the sloppy squeezeburger, the hot mess hug

Some hugs offer emotional support. This hug offers emotional and physical support. The form is more fluid—much like the huggers themselves. Drunken Hugs often last longer than other hugs, sometimes for several minutes or even the whole long walk home.

BEHIND THE BRO HUG

This classic two-parter starts as an interlocking hand clasp. Huggers lean their torsos together. The left hands are, of course, hitting the back. It's shake, hug, punch.

Few greetings are more intricate and nuanced than the North American Bro Hug. We call it the North American Bro Hug because many cultures have different norms for man-on-man signs of affection. According to Dr. Mark T. Morman, Professor of Graduate Studies at Baylor University, the Bro Hug is a product of our culture. "French, Italian, and South American men have a different conceptualization of masculinity," says Dr. Morman. "It is even very common for men in Middle Eastern cultures to hold hands."

In North America, it's not that simple. Dr. Morman explains, "When a man hugs another man, he is sending two messages: one to his friend and the other to any witnesses to the hug. To his friend he may be communicating affection, liking, appreciation, support, or encouragement—but to anyone watching, he is also communicating his masculinity."

So two men must take several different factors into consideration about landing a proper and acceptable embrace.

Coordination: It's important the two parties make their nonverbal intentions clear. Disaster lurks for those who don't coordinate their hug well.

Speed: Man hugs are tactical moves that are completed without wasted time or distraction. Go in, hug, get out.

Roughness: Men are generally rougher than women. Put two men together and a hug becomes close to a wrestling move. Why? Dr. Morman refers to it as covert affection, or "behaviors that don't look very affectionate, but in truth, really are."

Hitting: The ultimate hallmark of a man hug is the backslapping. It's important to ensure machismo is demonstrated at all times.

Never Hug from Behind: Approaching a huggee from behind can set off someone's fight-or-flight response, or at least scare the crap out of them. Unless the huggee is choking. Then it's totally cool.

KISSES

The kiss. There exists no other deeply intimate act that you can also do to a complete stranger. And while romantic and social kisses share some of the same body parts, the truth is, they have very different agendas.

HOW IT STARTED

Kissing runs deep. In our biology, that is. Zoologist Desmond Morris hypothesizes that the nurturing moments of breastfeeding are marked in our memory and make kissing a lifelong connection to feelings of safety and love. Of course, the fact that your lips are packed with tons of nerve endings helps. But how did the kiss become a social greeting? According to Daniel Akst, author of *We Have Met the Enemy: Self-Control in an Age of Excess*, "Social kissing might have evolved as a way for people to inoculate themselves against passion, as well as to demonstrate their ability to rein in or even transcend desire."

Which, of course, is very ironic because anyone who has struggled through a social kissing encounter that turns awkward knows the only desire is to get the whole thing over with. And quick.

HOW TO DO IT

A kiss is just a kiss—well, not really. A social kiss signals kindness, conviviality, and just a hint of poshness. A romantic kiss signals "me likey." A social kiss, when done right, spreads the positive spirit. A romantic kiss, when done wrong, spreads cold sores. So let's walk this fine line together.

Position Always go to the right side first. There are too many variables in executing a social kiss to debate which side. Just go right.

 Understand Consider the context of your relationship to the other person and the context of the culture. (See the following pages for a not-so-simple guide.)

 Cheek touch While there are many variations, it's often safest—socially and hygienically—to lightly touch cheeks. No actual lip contact required!

 Kiss air The moment you touch cheeks you should perform an air kiss. Some people make a kissing sound, some just purse their lips, and some just think kissing thoughts.

 Execute Depending on your culture, your kissee's culture, and everyone's overall openness to lip action, you will perform one, two, three, or even four kisses—alternate sides along the way.

 Retract When all is said and done and the kissing is complete, it's time to break the embrace and complete the greeting. At this stage, you may need to explain your kissing decisions. For example, "It's just that I lived in France for a semester, so I always kiss twice, officer. I hope that doesn't affect my ticket."

TYPES OF KISSES

Be warned: though technically chaste, some of these gestures are powerful, carrying the potential for confusion and blurred boundaries. On the other hand, the use of platonic kisses between lovers (or potential lovers) can make for flirtatious and/or romantic fun. Just a tip.

THE CHEEK PECK
aka: the K.I.S.S. kiss, the polite peck, the cheek-to-cheek

A simultaneous exchange of single cheek air kisses between two individuals is an acceptable form of greeting in nearly every culture. It's simple, nonthreatening, and virtually impossible to screw up. If only all things in life were this easy.

THE BLOWING KISS

aka: the love-you-all kiss, the crowd-pleaser, the let them eat kisses

The preferred form of greeting among tennis players, golfers, and well-coiffed pop stars, the Blowing Kiss is the perfect form of greeting when addressing a large and (hopefully) adoring crowd. Simply kiss your fingers and extend your arm in a long, sweeping gesture to the reverent multitudes around you.

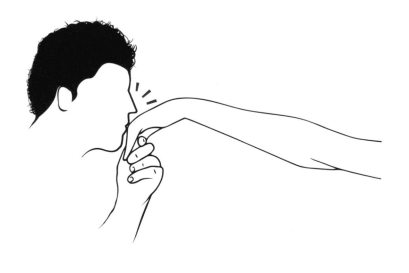

THE HAND KISS

aka: the m'lady kiss, the gotta hand it to you, the prim-and-proper peck

A staple among true gentlemen and power-wielding diplomats, the Hand Kiss occurs when a man gently holds and bows low over a woman's outstretched hand and lightly kisses the top of her knuckles. Although rare in this day and age, this elegant gesture indicates courtesy, respect, and fidelity. Come to think of it, those qualities are pretty rare these days, too.

GOING CHEEK TO CHEEK

Social kissing is like fried dough. Stay with us. Almost every culture enjoys it, but they put their own spin on the recipe. So here's a quick menu of the most common flavors of social kissing around the world.

Spain, Austria, Sweden, Italy: One kiss on each cheek, starting with the right.

France: Typically, two kisses—one on each cheek.

Belgium: Three kisses, particularly with anyone ten or more years your senior.

United Kingdom: Generally, a double kiss done with family/friends. (Doing it with anyone else is seen as odd and overly "French.")

Germany: Not touchy-feely types, Germans occasionally kiss but generally avoid it.

Philippines: A push of cheek to cheek (not lips to cheek).

Middle East: On the lips is the norm, but not between a man and woman.

Argentina: A single kiss, hello and goodbye, is the go-to greeting given to pretty much everyone.

Venezuela: A single kiss on the cheek, but only with close family and friends.

Eygpt, Russia: Three kisses.

Japan, China, Korea: Best to opt for a handshake or bow.

THE LIP KISS

aka: the uh-did-that-just-happen? kiss, the faux-pas peck, the social smooch

Actual platonic lip-locking is rare in a social setting, but it does indeed happen. Some people are surprisingly comfortable going full-on lip-to-lip. The key factors to an appropriate social kiss are that it's closed-mouth, dry, and quick. But in reality, the most important factor is simply personal confidence. Strike that: breath mints first, confidence second.

THE DOUBLE CHEEK KISS

aka: the other French kiss, le kiss-kiss, ooh-la-la lip service

When in France, do as the French do by planting a kiss on both cheeks of your recipient. This multipurpose greeting can be used to indicate friendship, to show respect, to offer congratulations, or because it's 2 PM on a Tuesday. Seriously, the French kiss a lot.

'SUP WITH MWAH?

Ever wonder about the sound you make when you air kiss? Many dictionaries list "mwah" as the official word—and sound effect—for the social kiss. Of course, this is not to be confused with "mwahaha," which is the official laugh of evil geniuses everywhere.

THE RING KISS

aka: the other Godfather *kiss, the kiss-up, the dead ringer*

There are some people for whom a simple handshake or kiss won't suffice. We're referring of course to the Pope, Mafia bosses, and anyone who can get you courtside seats at an NBA game. Should you ever meet one of these exalted individuals it's considered de rigueur to bend slightly and kiss the ring on their finger.

THE ESKIMO KISS

aka: the Nanook of the North, the follow your nose, the nose nuzzle

This cute nose-to-nose rub is actually a Western misinterpretation of the traditional Inuit greeting called a *kunik*. This greeting between family members involves pressing one's nose against the place you want to "kiss"—like a cheek—and breathing in.

'SUP WITH LONG KISSES?

The longest kiss award (at least for now) goes to Ekkachai Tiranarat and Laksana Tiranarat, who lip locked for over 58 hours in Pattaya, Thailand in 2013.

HIGH FIVE COMMANDMENT NO. 4
"THOU SHALT NOT LIMIT THE EXPRESSIONS OF
THE HANDS OR THE KNUCKLES."

CHAPTER 4

BUMPS & DAPS

It's now time to usher in a new era of hand communication where style, individuality, and forward thinking reign supreme—a renaissance of the hands and the knuckles.

Much like the hip-hop culture in which they've flourished, bumps and daps are bold, creative, and entirely misunderstood by older folks. But not us. As the Hand & Knuckle Society, we've been at the forefront of embracing the world of bumps and daps.

Sure, the fist can still be used in fisticuffs, but it's evolved into something much more palatable: an awesome instrument of positivity used to bump, pump, and thump our way into a peaceful society.

Did we mention it looks cool, too?

From athletes and politicians to biker gangs and germophobes, an alternative to the common handshake is becoming more commonplace in our ever-morphing society. So let's fully explore the new-school maneuvers that have quickly become the go-to for the hip and happening.

THE FIST BUMP

For much of its history the fist has been wrongly represented as an instrument of violence. Heck, Steven Seagal has his registered as deadly weapons.

While the fist can bring beat-downs and haymakers, it can also be used to bring about peaceful pounds and benevolent bumps. Where more formal gestures like the handshake were once the standard for unity, the fist bump has quickly usurped that title, offering friends and strangers alike a casual, noncommittal way to express solidarity, celebration, and amity to one another.

HOW IT STARTED

The fist bump has exploded on the scene—not unlike, well, an exploding fist bump. But when exactly was it born? A simple question without a simple answer. While its official origin is cloaked in mystery, several theories of the bump abound. But the most likely story is that it began in the center of the ring. The boxing ring, to be exact. Starting in the 1880s, boxers would touch knuckles to greet each other before the opening bell.

HOW TO DO IT

A fist bump can come across as a casual, totally awesome, in-the-moment greeting. And that's because it is! But it's also a gesture that requires some intricate maneuvers.

Focus A fist bump can turn into a fist punch if you're not careful. You need to commit to the bump and follow through. Don't be swayed by an invitation to shake.

Initiate Make your bumping intentions clear. Show your fist clearly, by angling it horizontally and facing your knuckles out. The bump initiator sets the agenda for the exchange.

Step Forward Although fist bumping could take place with outstretched arms, it's best delivered within a two-foot radius.

Tap Knuckles It all comes down to this: a quick, yet intentional touching of the knuckles. It should be done with enough force to make its presence known, but not enough to cause injury or, as participants say after being punched in the knuckles, "Holy crap that hurt. Why did you do that!?"

TYPES OF FIST BUMPS

As you've learned by now, most of the major greeting gestures have been around since antiquity. It's extremely rare to witness the emergence of a major new form of gesturing. We are lucky indeed, for we are witnesses to, and participants in, the proliferation of the fist bump. Your grandkids will be amazed.

THE CLASSIC BUMP

aka: knuckles, the global bump, the rookie, the k2k

This basic bump is a symmetrically aligned knuckle-to-knuckle greeting between both parties. Though typically performed using right hands, a classic bump can actually utilize either fist, right or left. This is the most universally used bump.

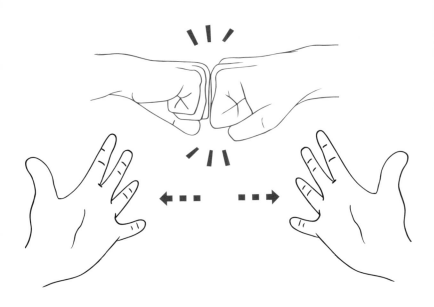

THE BLOWUP BUMP

aka: the exploding bump, the ka-BOOM bump, the big bang bump

This is an extension to the Classic Bump. After the fists touch, each party retracts their hands dramatically with fingers splayed. It's optional to make an explosion sound. For added flair exclaim, "Mashed potato, French fries!"

ALTERNATIVE FIST BUMP TERMINOLOGY

Knuckle Touch, Power Five, Pound, Fist Pound, Spudding, Fo' Knucks, Box, Bust, Spuds, Pound Dogg, Props, Bones, Respect Knuckles, Bumping the Rock, Brofist, Pound Cake, Sugar, Knuckle Crunching, Nudge

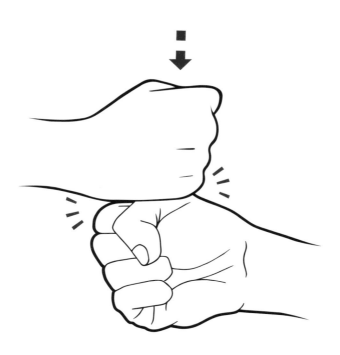

THE POUND

aka: potatoes, the double scoop, the dude bump

This is a twist to the bump—literally. Fists are turned
upright and the bumper comes down on top of the bumpee's
hand to make the connection. The bumpee then flips the
script and returns the pound back on top of the bumper's
fist. Boom, a brotastic greeting if ever there was one.

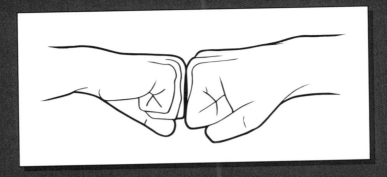

LET'S KEEP IT CLEAN

While the fist bump looks cool, it also serves a secondary purpose for many: to keep themselves as far as possible from the yucky bacteria and filth that reside on our hands.

Famously adopted by comedian, host, and celebrated germophobe Howie Mandel, the hygienically superior fist bump has gained popularity with the masses in recent years. And now science even backs up this practice. A 2014 study published in the *American Journal of Infection Control* showed that handshakes transfer ten times more bacteria than fist bumps (and two times more than high fives.)

With scientific evidence in their corner, many anti-germ advocates have actually proposed that society as a whole replace formal handshakes with fist bumps. While it may be hard to imagine, we could all be living in a future world where you can bump your boss, and North and South Korea may pound out a peace treaty. Dare to dream.

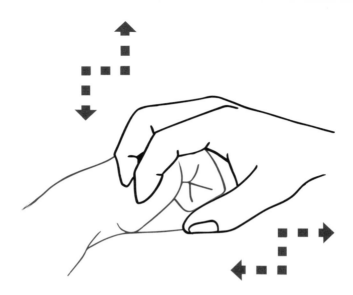

THE STICK-SHIFT BUMP

aka: the manual bump, the pedal-to-the-metal pound, the stick it to 'em, the Mario Andretti

When someone offers a fist to bump, but you want to crank things up a notch, try the Stick-Shift Bump. Grab their fist like you would a gearshift and start putting it through its paces. Extra points if you make a wicked awesome driving sound.

THINGS YOU SHOULD SAY TO GET A BUMP

Most of the time a bump can be elicited with a knowing glance. But it is important to know what to say when you need to ensure the other party is ready to bring the rock (a fist for bumping) instead of offering the paper (a hand for shaking).

☞ *Bump the rock.*
☞ *Gimme some pound cake.*
☞ *Respect.*

☞ *Come on, knuckle up.*
☞ *Let's just pound it out, Bro/Girl/Your Honor.*

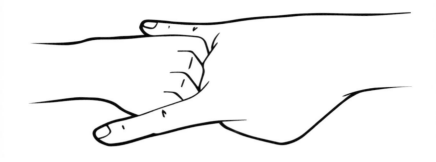

THE PARK THE CAR BUMP

aka: the park 'n' pound, the bumper bump, the Harvard yard

In this variation, one party makes a "parking space" by extending his index and pinky fingers. The other bumper then "parks" his fist between those fingers. A variation on this variation is the Parallel Parking Bump in which the person "misses" the space and then backs up into it.

THREE EPIC BUMPS

While some bumps pass like fists in the night, others have left their knuckle prints on history. Here are three epic examples.

Barack and Michelle Obama

Barack Obama doled out plenty of daps during his presidency, but none was more impactful than the fist bump he shared with his wife Michelle during a televised campaign speech on June 3, 2008. Dubbed "the fist bump heard 'round the world" by the *Washington Post*, the gesture upped Obama's cool quotient, and made him seem like a genuine man of the people.

Myron Lowery and the Dalai Lama

You really have nothing to lose when you're an interim mayor in a city like Memphis, TN. That's what Myron Lowery must have been thinking in 2009 when he welcomed His Holiness the Dalai Lama to the Home of the Blues by bumping fists and saying, "Hello, Dalai!" Depending upon your perspective it's either the greatest moment in the history of the fist bump, or the most deplorable moment in the history of international relations.

Baymax and Hiro in *Big Hero 6*

The words "fist bump" may not have been in Baymax's database initially, but they soon became an integral part of his world after Hiro introduced the gesture to him. The inflatable robot even added his own distinctive sound effect to make the gesture all his own. So kids around the world have been "Balalalala"-ing ever since.

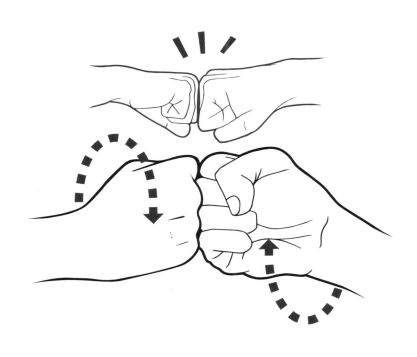

THE BUMP 'N' GRIND

aka: the pop 'n' lock, the pump 'n' pivot

There's certainly nothing wrong with adding a twist to the Classic Bump. In this case, quite literally. After initial knuckle contact, the fists turn ninety degrees, sealing in the greeting's freshness.

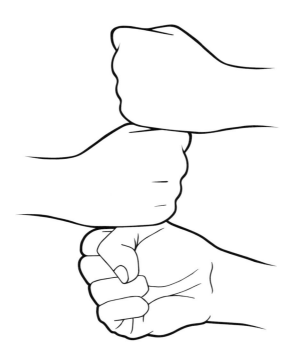

THE SNOWMAN

aka: Frosty the yo man, the triple play, the fist club sandwich

In this expansion of the pound, the bumpee doesn't return the pound but instead sandwiches the bumper's fist with his other fist to create a triple fist stack that recalls a snowman—or in this case, a snowbro.

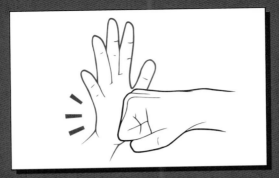

BUMPING MISHAPS

A well-timed, well-intentioned bump is the coolest of cool. A botched bump is the uncoolest of cool. Here are five common mishaps to avoid at any cost.

The Awkward Peacock: This beast is made from a high five and a bump coming together. Nothing pretty to say the least.

The Ball and Socket: This happens when one party offers a bump while the other goes in for the shake. The resulting awkward connection is painful . . . to watch.

The Limp Fist: When one party fails to commit and pulls up short, you get a Limp Fist Bump. This changes a forceful salutation into a weak tap of the hands.

The Jellyfish Bump: This is what happens when one party totally bails on the bump and tries to retreat with a partially opened fist and the fingers trailing. The resulting move looks like a fleeing jellyfish.

The Face Bump: The most egregious mishap is a fist bump to an unsuspecting face. This is one dumb move that really smarts.

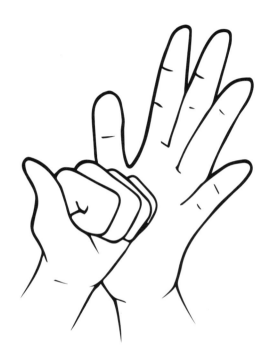

THE TURKEY BUMP

aka: the poultry pound, the gobbler, the Ben Franklin, the holiday hello

The Turkey Bump is a perfect treat for the holidays. To prep for this move, one person should open their hand up into a high five position, while the other makes a fist with the thumb extended like a hitchhiking sign. Put them together and you have a feast for your fists.

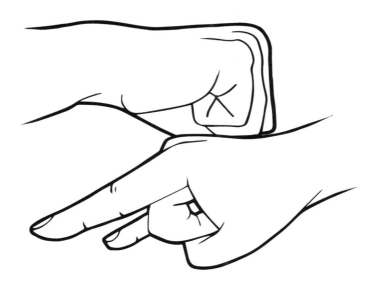

THE SNAIL BUMP

aka: the escar-bro bump, the gastropodian pound

This move involves one party avoiding the direct bump,
and placing his or her hand below the other party's fist and
extending the index and ring fingers to mimic a snail's body.

'SUP WITH THE LINGO?

While bumps have been officially cool for generations, it wasn't
"official English" until *Merriam-Webster* included the term in 2011.
Now that it's official, feel free to offer it up to your local librarian.

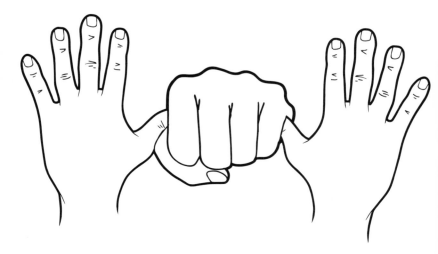

THE MOOSE

aka: the North American horned fist, the double Dutch boy, the Canadian salute

One person's fist remains, well, in a fist. The other party holds both hands splayed open with the thumbs stuck out and touching each side of his or her bump buddy's fist. The result is a fist bump worthy of mounting on the living room wall.

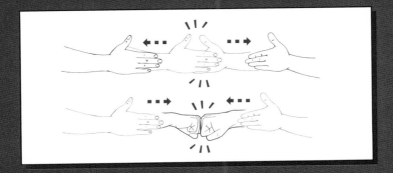

THE SKATER SLAP BUMP

While some group-oriented gestures can be used to greet outsiders, there are others that are used more to accept and signify someone as one of your own. The Slap Bump, often employed by skateboarders, is one of those gestures.

The gesture, which involves sliding the palms over each other and ending with a fist bump, is often only performed by skaters with other skaters among their ranks. As you can imagine, trust needs to be developed before being offered a Slap Bump, as noted by Gregory J. Snyder, sociologist and author of *Graffiti Lives: Beyond the Tag in New York's Urban Underground.*

"I learned this greeting the hard way when I began to do research on the West Coast with skaters," recalls Synder. "I expected to greet people with the more hip-hop centered East Coast dap, only to be given a firm, direct old man handshake. After I became more included in the culture I was greeted with the insiders' Slap Bump."

So while you may know the Slap Bump, being able use it among other skaters is a true rite of passage and a privilege—like so many other great gestures.

WHOLE BODY BUMPS

Why should fists get all the fun? Because they said so. They are fists, after all. But other than that, there is nothing stopping you from experimenting with other bumps all over your body.

The Chest Bump: A macho display performed by literally bumping one person's chest against the other, the Chest Bump is often executed as a form of extreme celebration. Once seen as a primal, testosterone-fueled release for exulting athletes, the Chest Bump can now be seen on the field, in the office, or anytime you get another round of complimentary breadsticks at your local Olive Garden.

The Reverse Back Bump: A close relative of the Chest Bump, the Reverse Back Bump was created for those seeking a little more variety and flair in their celebrations. The move involves two people jumping into the air toward one another and spinning at the right moment to make their backs collide. This high-risk maneuver looks great when done correctly, and cringe-worthy when done awkwardly.

The Forearm Bash: A revved-up version of the fist bump, the Forearm Bash involves both people crashing the outer parts of their forearms into one another as a form of celebration. Made popular by the Bash Brothers—juiced-up Major League Baseball players Mark McGwire and Jose Canseco—in the late 1980s, the Forearm Bash became a slightly more aggressive replacement for the standard high five.

The Forehead Bump: Performed when two people carefully press the tops of their foreheads together, this is a bump divided. If done gently, it works for more heartfelt occasions—like greeting an old friend. If done with intensity, it can be used by football players or professional wrestlers to celebrate by inflicting pain on their teammates.

The Elbow Bump: In 2006 when Avian flu panic swept the globe, the World Health Organization advocated use of the Elbow Bump as an alternative to the handshake. Like the fist bump, it prevents the spread of germs caused by actual pressing of the filthy, filthy flesh. And it's simple—just point your elbow toward the person you're greeting and gently bump theirs with yours.

The Hip Bump: While most body-part bumps are performed as a greeting or celebration, the Hip Bump is meant for one thing: gettin' your groove on. Typically seen in a variety of dance crazes, the Hip Bump involves two part-ners rhythmically bumping side booties. This move was all the rage during the 1970s and makes frequent comebacks on the dance floor during wedding receptions and bar mitzvahs the world over.

The Underwater Butt Bump: Performed primarily by children, this maneu-ver involves two people each holding the other's hands, then submerging beneath the surface of a pool. Pressing the feet together and bending at the knees causes the two butts to swing down and make contact. Of course, you can try this as an adult, too, if you can find a willing partner.

DAPS

The dap is more of a ritual than a single greeting. It might involve fist bumps, high fives, snaps, slaps, and other moves. But it is rarely spontaneous. Rather it's a choreographed series of gestures and symbols that show camaraderie and respect.

HOW IT STARTED

Some attribute dapping to African-American soldiers during the Vietnam War as a way of demonstrating solidarity. Others attribute it to the 1960s civil rights movement. And while the claim that it's an acronym for "Dignity and Pride" is likely erroneous, the spirit is 100% correct.

According to sociologist and author Gregory J. Snyder, the early version of the dap was relatively standard. "This greeting involved a hand-to-hand 'soul clasp,' followed by placing the arm on another's shoulder in a show of solidarity and respect followed by a reemphasis of the soul clasp and ending with the fist in the air black power salute."

HOW TO DO IT

The infinite possibility of the dap can be a challenge for those who like hard-and-fast rules. But proponents of the hip-hop handshake enjoy its flexibility. The dap can be quick, or it can be an elaborate series of synchronized manuevers, but either way it always has to have style. Now go express yourself, please.

Decide Because of the intricate and symbolic nature of the gesture, it's essential that you determine whether a potential dap partner is truly worthy of your respect.

 Approach Signal your dap intentions by extending an open hand from the side, thumb extended, with fingers curled together and slightly cupped.

 Palms You and your dap partner should encircle each other's thumbs while establishing the all-important palm-to-palm contact. At its heart, this really is a handshake, after all.

 Solidarity Mutually clasp each other's hands with bent fingers and a solid grip. This is about you both affirming each other as deep comrades, almost like family.

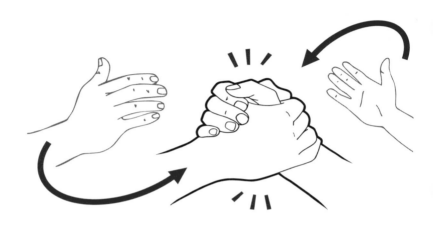

THE BASIC DAP
aka: the cup, the soul clasp, the dap 101

This modern-day remix of the handshake has been embraced by cool kids and athletes worldwide. Hold the hand in a "c" formation with the thumb extended, then meet and clasp hands for a beat or two. It's important that the sound be sharp and hollow upon contact, which is a sign of proper respect and execution. This maneuver can lead to a back slap or a full-on man hug.

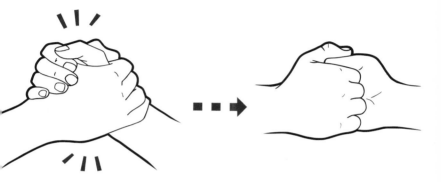

THE DAP GRIP

aka: the 1-2, the dap 2.0, the slap 'n' snap

This common expansion of the dap is the perfect addition to your
dap game. Start with the Basic Dap and transition by sliding into
a tight finger grip. It just feels so natural and easily opens up to
a series of full dap add-ons like a Bro Hug, a pound, a mutual
finger pull-n-snap, or even just a thumb-wrestling match.

HIGH FIVE COMMANDMENT NO. 5
"NEVER LEAVE ANYONE HANGING."

CHAPTER 5

LOW & HIGH FIVES

All hail the fives—the low ones, the high ones, the group ones, the solo ones. The five is the perfect combination of both salutation and festivity. And for that reason, it has become the foundation of the Hand & Knuckle Society.

As fives have grown in popularity, they run the risk of becoming commonplace—less valued, less special, and unfortunately less likely to be executed. And the five not given may result in egregious errors, like the painful act of leaving someone hanging. Not only does this break the commandments of our secret society, but it breaks the fabric of our greater society. Well, at least it hurts some feelings.

So let's focus on the positive power of fives in all of their forms, and welcome the gesture with open minds, hearts, and palms.

THE LOW FIVE

Before the high five, the low five was just, well, the five. While the low five doesn't sport the bravado of its elevated brethren, it's impossible to deny that this cooler cousin to the handshake represents an important step in human nonverbal communication. Its appearance quite possibly marks the first time a greeting was more cool than formal, and more style than ceremony. So it's time we all gave it up for the low five.

HOW IT STARTED

Although its exact pedigree is fuzzy, all signs point to its birth in the hazy smoke of jazz clubs. Some theorize that the low five started as a secret greeting between musicians to let each other know they were hip to the scene. And because it's simple to perform with panache, it was perfect for sharing on stage as well.

Giving five—or "slappin' skin"—was immortalized for the whole world by Al Jolson in the 1927 film *The Jazz Singer*. Later it took top billing in the Andrews Sisters' 1941 hit "Gimme Some Skin, My Friend." And while it reached its peak with the jazz era, it's still alive and well today with cool people of all musical persuasions.

HOW TO DO IT

Giving and receiving proper fives involves five fingers (sorry, Jerry Garcia) and a five-letter acronym that just happens to spell "F-I-V-E-S"—and even more coincidentally contains the five steps to perfect execution of the fives. That's a lot of fives.

Flat Keep your hands open and horizontal—palm up to receive the five, palm down to give. This horizontal position of the hands is the key feature of a low five, so keep it nice and flat.

Initiate Contact Start by presenting your hand horizontally with the palm facing up, at waist level. Establish eye contact with your potential fiving partner.

Verbalize Traditionally, the initiator utters an invitational phrase such as "Gimme five!" or "Give me some skin."

Extend It Out Extend your receiving hand forward in a smooth motion toward your fiving friend. Remember to keep it chill and cool.

Slap Smooth Save the hard smacking for the drums. Instead, bring your hand down nice and easy for a quick slap with a subtle pull-away immediately after contact.

TYPES OF LOW FIVES

The high five may be the alpha dog, but the low five has a more subtle charm, greater capacity for nuance, and blurs the boundaries pleasantly between salutation and schoolyard-style game.

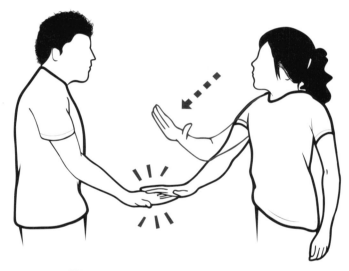

THE STANDARD LOW FIVE

aka: slap skin, humble five'n it, the no-frills fiver, the sweet 'n' low

This is a simple palm-to-palm slap—no flourishes, no smacking sounds, no second moves. Just a workhorse greeting that says, "Hey, that was awesome."

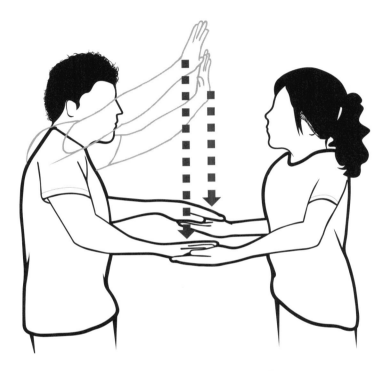

THE DOUBLE LOW FIVE
aka: the low ten, the double dawg, the two-fer

Simultaneous performance of two low fives. Often paired
with "Oh, yeah." or "*That's* what I'm talking about."

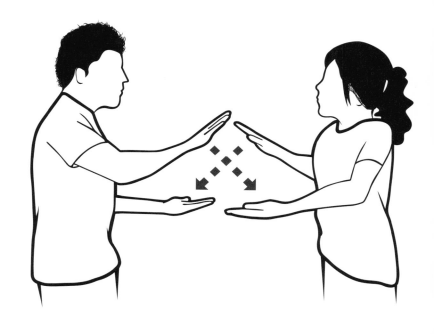

THE PLAYGROUND PAT-PAT

aka: the five by five, the double-dutch five

In this two-handed greeting, one hand is giving a five, while the other is simultaneously receiving one. The process is then repeated on the other side. This takes a little planning and rehearsal, which is why it's perfectly suited to the playground.

HIGH AND LOW FIVE PRANKS

These shenanigans violate everything the high five is about: bonding, friendship, and lots of trust. But they are funny. So when it comes down to it, punk all you want.

The Up High, Down Low, In the Middle, Too Slow

Also known within the Hand & Knuckle Society as HLM2S, this is a classic prank that never gets old—or any less frustrating to young fivers. The pranker lulls the prankee into an unassuming routine: a high five, a low five, and ostensibly a middle five. At this point, the prankster says "too slow" before pulling his hand away in soul-crushing jest.

Cut the Pickle, Tickle Tickle

An endearing version of the prank above, the prankster does the full series (up high, down low, in the middle), then she places her index fingers together and invites the prankee to "cut the pickle" with a chop or finger scissor movement. After said pickle is cut, the pranker surprises the prankee by saying, "tickle, tickle," and tickles the prankee's neck area, or other ticklish zone.

The Psych

This prank is also designed to make someone whiff on purpose. We know, it's almost too tragic to consider. The prankster approaches the prankee with the palm-up international symbol for high five. Before contact is made, the prankster moves his hand away—often running it through his hair—and says, "Psyyyyych!," leaving the prankee fiveless and dejected.

THE RETURN LOW FIVE
aka: the five and five, the right back at ya

In the Hand & Knuckle Society, we refer to this is as a reciprocal and reflective matching application of the Standard Low Five. But you can call it the Return Low Five. This is the trading of low fives where the receiver returns the favor by switching positions and giving it back with another five.

THE FIVE & DIME
aka: the hustle, the payola palmer, the secret slip, the FIFA

This is a low five where the palm of the top hand discreetly holds an object that gets passed surreptitiously to the receiver. Best used in a cool heist movie or when passing notes in class.

THE MOVING LOW HIGH FIVE
aka: the entrance, the starting lineup, the helloooo five

Whether you're entering a stadium to play before thousands or entering the dance floor as husband and wife, this is the five for you. It requires a line of hands held at or below waist level. Bending down as you move down the line gives you a perfect runway for your big moment.

NOT REALLY A SLAM DUNK

In 2010, a clip of a botched low five between two Minnesota Timberwolves players went viral, prompting the release of a parody video calling the mishap one of the "most tragic moments in Minnesota sports history." In it, the players lament their lack of skill and are forced to do daily "game-time handshake" training sessions. (Unfortunately, this book had yet to be written.)

THE LOUD LOW
aka: the slam slap, the heck yeah!, the goes-up-to-eleven low

This a low five delivered with authority—often given after a strike is bowled or a presentation is nailed. If it had happened in history (and we're not saying it did), it may have accompanied Julius Caesar's *veni, vidi, vici*—a succinct statement, in slap form.

THE PET FIVE
aka: gimme paw, cat pat, the furry fiver

Extending your hand out for a little furry one to pat it is a great form of cross-species communication. There's nothing cuter than connecting with our four-legged (or fine-feathered) friends.

THE SKIN AND SLIDE
aka: the jazz five, the can you dig it?, the Thelonius Monk

A throwback to its jazzy origins, this low five comes with an extended and pronounced slide after initial contact. Can be finished with a snap or simply a knowing glance to your bandmate after a sweet solo.

THINGS YOU SHOULD SAY TO GET A LOW FIVE

While the low five can work nonverbally, it's useful to alert your partner it's time to trade some skin. Here are six certified things to say in this instance.

☞ *Gimme some skin.*
☞ *Slap me some skin.*
☞ *Gimme five.*

☞ *Down low.*
☞ *Bring it on down.*
☞ *Right?!*

THE HIGH FIVE

It's the highest of all fives, and an expression of unbridled joy. It's an explosion of happiness and a nonverbal embodiment of the Kool-Aid guy crashing through the wall.

The contagious awesomeness, the immediate sense of satisfaction, the cool camaraderie, the victory of teamwork—these are just some of the unparalleled joys a high five brings to the world.

HOW IT STARTED

It's clear that the high five evolved naturally from its low-hanging cousin. Exactly how it happened has a murky tangle of different accounts and claims, but one of the most prominent theories is that it was born in a spontaneous moment at the end of the regular baseball season in 1977, when Dodger Glenn Burke went to congratulate Dusty Baker for his 30th homerun. While the gesture may or may not have been new, many consider this event as birthing the term "high five." The gesture quickly caught on, to the point where the Dodgers began selling high five T-shirts and marketing themselves as the creators of the hand-on-hand celebration. To this day, Burke is often celebrated more for the invention of the high five than he is for any of his athletic accomplishments.

HOW TO DO IT

Time to take your hand to the next level: high above your head, to be exact. That most supreme slap—and the one that gave this handbook its title— is a party wrapped inside two palms. Are you ready to get high, real high?

Hand Raise your hand proudly to eye level to initiate the high five with wrist firm, fingers stretched, and palm open.

 Eyes Make eye contact to confirm initiation, but as you make your approach, aim your eyes at your fellow high fiver's elbow to properly align palms with perfection.

 Go Extend your arm and launch your palm up, out, and forward, making certain you focus on direct and solid contact with the other party's palm.

 Hit As you reach the top of your arc of motion, cup your palm ever so slightly to achieve the maximum clapping sound and then . . . BOOM! Make solid palm-to-palm contact at the peak for a precisely timed thunderclap.

TYPES OF HIGH FIVES

When you high five another person, you are invoking a mysterious primal power, tapping into a universal energy frequency accessible only through high fiving. Unleashed on a global scale, this power could save the planet.

THE BASIC HIGH FIVE
aka: the high 5.0, semper five

This classic is a simple palm-to-palm slap executed at eye level between two people. There is just enough forward movement to make contact and spark the party. Like a black dress or Bill Murray, it never goes out of style.

THE DOUBLE HIGH FIVE

aka: high ten, four hands good, the dynamic duo

Some moments are too cool for just one five. This double clap
of awesome usually occurs above the shoulder line for better
visibility and twice the sound—and twice the attention.

THINGS YOU SHOULD SAY TO GET A HIGH FIVE

☞ *High five!*
☞ *Up high!*
☞ *Cinco de Palmo!*
☞ *Give it up!*
☞ *Don't leave me hanging!*

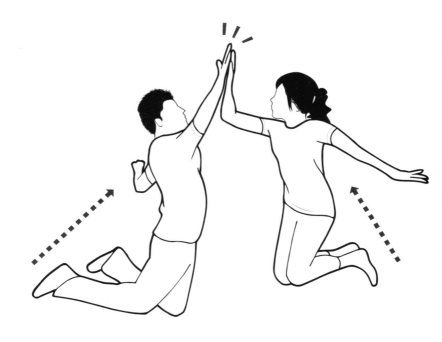

THE JUMP FIVE

aka: higher fiver, the high hop, the high flier

Experts combine a jump and a slap for increased elevation
and awesomeness. This takes extra coordination with your
partner to both meet midair. While it might require some
practice, a properly executed Jump Five is a thing of beauty.

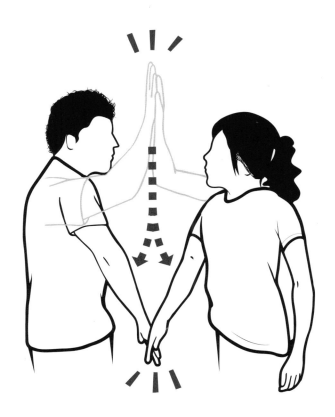

THE TOP GUN

aka: the high low, the up and under, the shirtless slap slap

**No high five better captures the essence of the 1980s than the
ol' "up and under" hand slaps exchanged by Maverick and Goose
during the volleyball scene in *Top Gun*. It's a Basic High Five with
a follow-through that connects with an upside-down high five.**

EPIC FIVES

Some people are born great. Others have greatness thrust upon them. And sometimes what is thrust upon them is an outstretched palm waiting to be slapped. These are those thrustings.

Kelly Slater Surf Five

The surf legend received a massive five from fellow competitor (and close friend) Rob Machado at the 1995 Pipe Masters. Exiting his own barrel during the semi-finals, Machado was in prime position to take priority, but instead he carved out a huge turn directly toward Slater and gave him a high five as the champ awaited his turn. Fans dubbed it "the high five heard 'round the world."

First Ever Sky Five

Australian BASE jumper Nathan J. Jones donned a wingsuit and "flew" off a mountain in the Alps. Skimming above the trees and boulders, he made contact with a foam hand held up by a teammate. The stunt raised awareness for both a charitable project to build a well in Africa and the worthy cause of high five awareness.

Ryan Seacrest High Fives a Blind Guy

Epic doesn't necessarily mean positive. The *American Idol* host unintentionally alerted the nation to the plague of high five failing when he tried to five a blind competitor early in the show's run. Seacrest then made an uncomfortable situation even more unbearable by seizing the competitor's hand and forcing the high five upon him. It stands as one of the most awkward moments in television history.

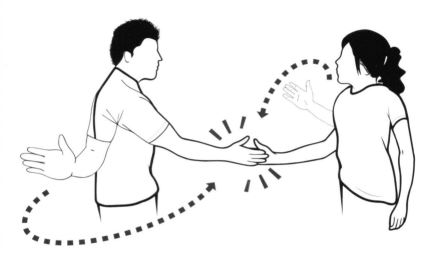

THE SIDE FIVE
aka: the magic, the yeah boy!

Less showy, more intimate, this high five involves motion of
the arms in a cross-body swipe with a mid-level connection
point. Good friends can double up and slap twice. Best
friends go from this five to a dap, then to a Bro Hug.

THE NO-LOOK FIVE

aka: front seat fiver, the alley-oop five

Most high fives build trust. This one requires it. When a
partner is sitting in front of the other—in a class or car or
courtroom, the front partner executes a blind over-the-
shoulder palm-out move. And the back partner connects.

FIVING MISHAPS

When a high five goes right, pure excitement—not just hands—hits the air. When they go wrong, the you-know-what hits the fan. Here are the most common mishaps that can happen to the best of us.

Left Hanging: This is a mishap of miscommunication where one partner is left with hand in ready position but no one to five with. One of the most famous instances of this was when the New England Patriot's quarterback Tom Brady was left hanging by his teammates, leaving him embarrassed and, um, deflated.

Tipping and Whiffing: This happens when there is an intention to five but the execution fails. A tip is when the hands touch in a sloppy, incomplete manner. A whiff, on the other hand, is a complete miss of the other hand. Said differently, it is the air ball of fiving.

Face Five/Eye Five: If the other mishaps hurt the ego, this hurts the body, too. An off-target five can easily land in the face, head, or neck region of the recipient. Sad that something so cool can cause something so uncool.

The Stinger: Sometimes you can have too much of a good thing, especially if the good thing is high-speed, skin-on-skin slapping. Not only does excess slapping hurt in the moment, it can make the slappee wary to five in the future. And that is the greatest sin of all.

THE FOOT FIVE

aka: the look ma! no hands, the lowest five, the My Left Foot *five*

There are some occasions where our hands are simply not available for fiving, whether they are holding stuff, carrying stuff, or just covered in, you know, stuff. These are the times our other digits (i.e., our toes) can tag in. As Kid 'n Play showed us during their raging '90s house parties, using our feet as props to give, well, props is a true art form.

THE FIVE NO-FIVE ZONES

1. Funeral
2. Urinal
3. Operating room
4. Juror box
5. None, there are literally no other places a high five is not acceptable.

THE SOLO FIVE

aka: the selfie fivie, my five, the party-of-one palmer, the Hand Solo

If self-help books have taught us one thing, it's to respect your spirit animal. If they taught us two things, it's to love yourself. Sometimes that requires a Solo Five. So when you're with your party of one, feel free to serve up your own celebration.

'SUP WITH THE HIGH FIVE HOLIDAY?

National High Five Day was started in 2002 at the University of Virginia. Now people of all ages celebrate the day by giving high fives to friends, coworkers, and strangers. So put it up high on the third Thursday of April every year.

THE FRESH PRINCE FIVE
aka: the slap snap, the you know!

This is a Side Five that flows seamlessly into a lean back with a snap. Parents might not understand this move, but the cool kids do. Works equally well in both West Philadelphia and Bel Air.

THE AIR FIVE
aka: the wi-five, the long five, the phony phive

When partners are standing too far apart, an Air Five is the perfect solution. To ensure it is not confused with a mere wave, both parties need to "push air" in the direction of the other to create a symbolic five action.

THE FREEZE FRAME FIVE
aka: the credits roll five, the very-special-episode five, the canned five

We all know if it's on TV, it must be true. And nothing concludes a sitcom episode like a group high five that freezes while the credits roll. But you don't need to be on TV or attend Bayside High to do it on your own. Just hold your pose for between five seconds and eleven minutes. Blinking is optional but not encouraged.

'SUP WITH INJURIES?

According to the Bleacher Report, 1980s Atlanta Braves outfielder Terry Harper injured his shoulder while giving a teammate a high five.

HOW TO RECOVER FROM BEING LEFT HANGING

There are many significant pains in life: childbirth, heartbreak, anything involving a mule's kick. But one of the most unforgettable pains is that of being left hanging. Holding your hand out for a five and being denied is very sad indeed.

Here are a few ways to save face when saving your hand.

☞ Pretend you were fixing your hair.

☞ Go straight to a fist pump.

☞ Keep your hand out and start to wave.

☞ Keep your hand up and say, "Excuse me, I have a question."

☞ Act like you were swatting a fly.

☞ Shoot an imaginary jump shot and hold your follow-through.

☞ Pretend to hail a cab if outside on the street.

☞ Keep your hand out and give the finger to the person who left you hanging. (You know who you are, Carl.)

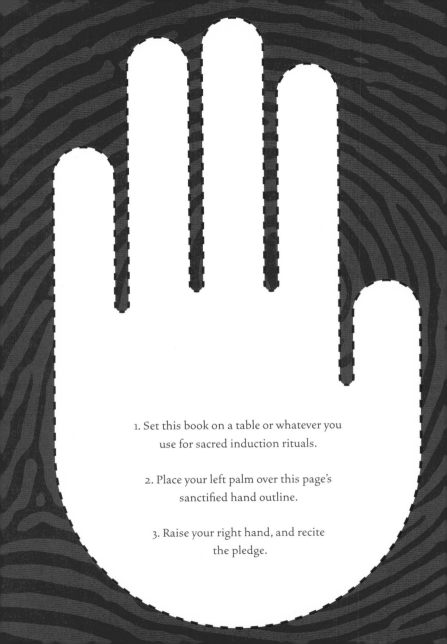

1. Set this book on a table or whatever you use for sacred induction rituals.

2. Place your left palm over this page's sanctified hand outline.

3. Raise your right hand, and recite the pledge.